Questions and Answers: Countries

Egypt

by Christine Webster

Consultant:
Barbara Petzen, Outreach Coordinator
Center for Middle Eastern Studies
Harvard University
Cambridge, Massachusetts

Capstone
press

Mankato, Minnesota

Fact Finders is published by Capstone Press
151 Good Counsel Drive, P.O. Box 669, Mankato, Minnesota 56002
www.capstonepress.com

Library of Congress Cataloging-in-Publication Data
Webster, Christine.
    Egypt / by Christine Webster.
    p. cm.—(Fact finders. Questions and answers: Countries)
    Includes bibliographical references and index.
    ISBN 0-7368-2688-2 (hardcover)
    1. Egypt—Juvenile literature. I. Title. II. Series.
DT49.W43 2005
962—dc22   2004000779

Summary: A brief introduction to Egypt, following a simple question-and-answer format
    that discusses land features, government, housing, transportation, industries,
    education, sports, art forms, holidays, food, and family life. Includes a map, fast facts,
    and charts.

Editorial Credits
Erika L. Shores, editor; Kia Adams, series designer; Jennifer Bergstrom, book designer;
    maps.com, map illustrator; Wanda Winch, photo researcher; Scott Thoms, photo editor;
    Eric Kudalis, product planning editor

Photo Credits
AP/Wide World Photos, 9; Bruce Coleman Inc./Jennifer Elsayed Omar, 26–27; Bruce
Coleman Inc./Luis Villota, 15; Bruce Coleman Inc./Malcolm Hanes, 12; Corbis/Aladin
Abdel Naby, 23; Corbis/Kevin Fleming, 16–17; Corbis/Reuters NewMedia Inc., 19; Corbis
Royalty-Free, cover (both), 21; Flat Earth, 1; Getty Images/Hulton Archive, 7; Getty
Images/Mark Wilson, 8; John Elk III, 4, 11, 13, 25, 29 (top); StockHaus Limited, 29 (bottom);
TRIP/B. North, 16

1 2 3 4 5 6 09 08 07 06 05 04

Table of Contents

Features

Where is Egypt?

Egypt is a country in northeast Africa. It is about three times the size of the U.S. state of New Mexico.

The world's longest river flows through Egypt. The Nile River flows north to the Mediterranean Sea. Near the sea, the Nile spreads out to make the Nile **Delta**.

Sailboats travel along the Nile River in Egypt. ➤

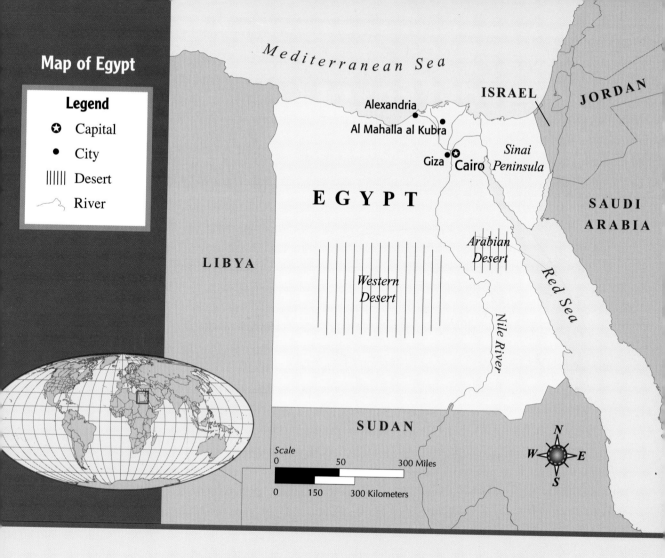

Map of Egypt

Legend
- ✪ Capital
- • City
- ||||| Desert
- ⌇ River

Mediterranean Sea

ISRAEL

JORDAN

Alexandria

Al Mahalla al Kubra

Sinai Peninsula

Giza ✪ Cairo

EGYPT

SAUDI ARABIA

LIBYA

Arabian Desert

Western Desert

Red Sea

Nile River

SUDAN

Scale
0   50   300 Miles

0   150   300 Kilometers

N W E S

Deserts are the main landform in Egypt. The Western Desert region is part of the huge Sahara Desert. The Sahara covers much of northern Africa. The Eastern Desert region of Egypt also is called the Arabian Desert.

When did Egypt become a country?

Egypt became an independent country in 1953. Before 1953, other countries and nations controlled Egypt. Over thousands of years, groups including the Greeks and Romans ruled ancient Egyptians. The British took control in 1882. They were the last group to control the area. In 1952, a **revolution** led by Gamal Abdel Nasser ended British rule in Egypt. In 1954, Nasser became Egypt's first president.

Fact!

In 1971, Egypt's president Anwar al-Sadat made the Arab Republic of Egypt the country's official name.

Gamal Abdel Nasser was Egypt's first president.

Egypt is one of the world's oldest **civilizations**. People have lived in Egypt for at least 5,000 years. An Egyptian **legend** says a king called Narmer formed the world's first national government in Egypt in 3100 BC.

What type of government does Egypt have?

Egypt is a **republic**. In a republic, people elect a president and a legislature to run the country. Egypt's president selects a group of advisers called a cabinet. A **prime minister** leads the cabinet. The cabinet helps the president run the country.

Hosni Mubarak became Egypt's president in 1981. ➤

Egypt's People's Assembly has 444 members.

Egypt's legislature is called the People's Assembly. People in Egypt's 26 districts elect leaders to represent them in the People's Assembly. The Assembly has some power. But the president has most of the power to make plans and decisions for Egypt.

What kind of housing does Egypt have?

Many Egyptians live in homes made of concrete or mud-brick near the Nile River. Most are farmers growing food crops or cotton. These people are called fellahin.

Egypt's cities are crowded. Cairo, Egypt's capital, is the largest city. Almost 20 million people live in Cairo and its nearby areas.

Where do people in Egypt live?

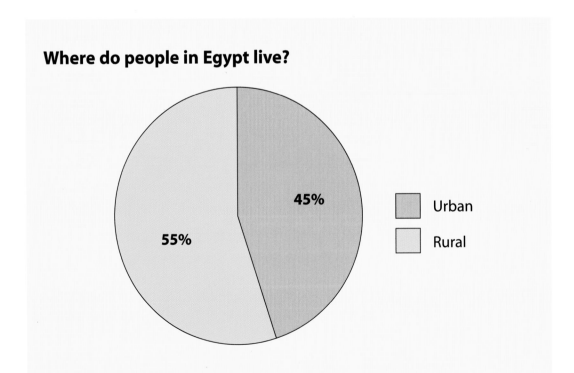

45%

55%

Urban

Rural

*Tall apartment buildings
are home to many people
in Egypt's capital, Cairo.*

In Cairo, rich people live in apartment
buildings or modern houses. The poor
live in small crowded apartments. Some
people live in huts built on the roofs of
apartment buildings.

What are Egypt's forms of transportation?

Egyptians have many different ways to travel. Highways and railroads join cities. Egyptians ride buses, trains, cars, motorcycles, and bikes. Outside the cities, Egyptians also use donkeys and sometimes camels.

These Egyptians offer camel rides to tourists. Tourists can ride camels to see ancient sites. ▶

People drive cars through Cairo's busy streets.

Some Egyptians use airplanes and boats to travel. Planes from around the world fly into Cairo's airport. Alexandria is the leading **port** on the Mediterranean Sea. Boats there carry goods and people.

What are Egypt's major industries?

Egypt's service **industry** leads the country in jobs. Half of Egypt's workers have jobs providing a service to one another. These jobs include teaching, banking, and selling.

Manufacturing provides jobs in the cities. Workers make steel, cement, clothing, and food products. Egypt ships these goods to many countries.

What does Egypt import and export?	
Imports	**Exports**
chemicals	cotton
food products	oil
machinery and equipment	textiles

Farmers use animals to pull plows through their fields.

In rural areas, agriculture is the main industry. Farmers grow cotton, corn, and potatoes. They also grow fruits and vegetables. Egypt is one of the largest growers of dates in the world.

What is school like in Egypt?

In Egypt, most children age 6 to 14 go to school. Egypt's government pays for school for all children.

Some schools in Egypt have too many students. As a result, some students go to classes only in the morning. Other students then go to school in the afternoon.

Egypt's government wants to improve schools across the country. In some areas, new schools have been built. ▶

Children in Egypt learn to read and write Arabic.

Some children cannot go to school at all. They are needed at home to help their families earn money. Children may work in the fields or in factories.

Some students attend a university after high school. Egypt has 13 universities.

What are Egypt's favorite sports and games?

Egypt's most popular sport is soccer. People play soccer in cities and towns across Egypt. People go to see local matches. School soccer teams compete against each other. Many Egyptians also enjoy watching pro soccer games on TV.

Other sports and games are popular in Egypt. Many people enjoy playing volleyball, tennis, and basketball.

Fact!

Paintings on the walls of tombs show that ancient Egyptians took part in many sporting events. Wrestling, boxing, and ball games were common sports played in ancient Egypt.

Many people play board and card games in Egypt. Backgammon and checkers are popular throughout the country. Checkers was invented in Egypt. Bridge is a popular card game in Egypt.

What are the traditional art forms in Egypt?

Egyptians today enjoy many art forms. Literature, music, and films are popular. Egyptian author Naguib Mahfouz won the **Nobel Prize** for literature in 1988. He was the first Arabic writer to win this honor. Poetry is also popular in Egypt. Egyptians enjoy reading poems and singing. Many films are made in Egypt.

Fact!

Egypt's Valley of the Kings has 64 tombs of ancient Egyptian kings. King Tutankhamen's tomb is the only one that was never robbed. More than 1,700 pieces of sculpture, jewelry, and pottery were found in King Tut's tomb.

Huge pyramids still stand in Egypt today.

In Egypt, traditional art forms included sculpture and **architecture**. Ancient Egyptians built huge pyramids as tombs for some of their kings. Today, people learn about ancient Egypt from treasures and art found inside these tombs.

What major holidays do people in Egypt celebrate?

Most Egyptians follow the Islamic religion. Many holidays center around this religion. Ramadan is an important time for Muslims. During the month of Ramadan, Muslims do not eat during the daytime. After sundown, people eat a meal with family and friends.

At the end of Ramadan, Muslims celebrate Eid al-Fitr. Children receive new clothes to wear. They eat sugar cookies filled with nuts.

What other holidays do people in Egypt celebrate?

Coptic Christians in Egypt celebrate the following holidays:
Christmas
Easter
Saints' Day

People fill Cairo's streets to celebrate Eid al-Fitr. The holiday marks the end of Ramadan.

Egypt's national holiday is Revolution Day. This day honors the 1952 revolution. The holiday is celebrated on July 23. Fireworks and parades are part of the celebration.

What are the traditional foods of Egypt?

Meals including bread and beans are common in Egypt. Egyptians eat stewed fava beans almost every day. They call this dish *fuul*.

Other meals include rice, pasta, and vegetables. Okra is common in soups and stews. Okra is a green pod from the okra plant.

Fact!

Karkadeh *is a favorite drink during Ramadan. This drink is made from dried flower petals. It is served hot or cold.*

Egyptians sell fresh fruits and vegetables at markets.

Eggplant is often used in Egyptian dishes. One common eggplant dish is baba ghanouj. This dish combines sesame seeds and ground eggplant.

What is family life like in Egypt?

Many Egyptian families are large. Some families live together in big buildings in the city. Grandparents, aunts, uncles, and cousins often live in apartments in the same building. Families usually eat a meal together at night.

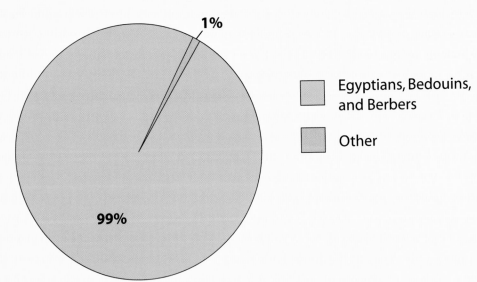

What are the ethnic backgrounds of people in Egypt?

1%

99%

Egyptians, Bedouins, and Berbers

Other

Children sometimes join their parents on trips to outdoor markets.

Children in Egypt spend their free time playing sports or other games. Many children in Egypt play soccer after school and on weekends. Girls and boys often play hopscotch on city sidewalks.

Egypt Fast Facts

Official name:

Arab Republic of Egypt

Land area:

386,660 square miles
(1,001,449 square
kilometers)

**Average annual
precipitation (Cairo):**

1 inch (2.5 centimeters)

**Average January
temperature (Cairo):**

57 degrees Fahrenheit
(14 degrees Celsius)

**Average July
temperature (Cairo):**

82 degrees Fahrenheit
(28 degrees Celsius)

Population:

74,718,797 people

Capital city:

Cairo

Language:

Arabic

Natural Resources:

iron ore, natural gas, petroleum

Religions:

Islamic	94%
Coptic Christian	6%

Money and Flag

Money:

Egypt's money is the Egyptian pound. In 2004, 1 U.S. dollar equaled about 6 pounds and 1 Canadian dollar equaled 4.7 pounds .

Flag:

Egypt's flag has three equal bands of red, white, and black. The red band stands for revolution. The white band stands for Egypt's bright future. The black band represents its past. The golden eagle stands for the Muslim ruler Saladin. He ruled during the 1100s.

Learn to Speak Arabic

People in Egypt speak Arabic. The letters in the Arabic alphabet do not look like those in the English alphabet. Some Arabic words are written here in the English alphabet.

American	Arabic	Pronunciation
hello	marhaba	(MAR-hab-ah)
good-bye	ma'a s-salama	(MAH-ah sah-LAH-mah)
please	min fadlak	(MIHN FAHD-lahk)
thank you	shukran	(SHUH-krahn)
yes	aywa	(EYE-wah)
no	laa	(LAH)

Glossary

architecture (AR-ki-tek-chur)—the planning and designing of buildings

civilization (siv-i-luh-ZAY-shuhn)—an organized and advanced society

delta (DEL-tuh)—the triangle-shaped area where a river deposits mud, sand, and pebbles as it enters the sea

industry (IN-duh-stree)—a single branch of business or trade

legend (LEJ-uhnd)—a story handed down from earlier times

Nobel Prize (NOH-bell PRYZ)—an award given to someone for earning the highest honor in their field; Naguib Mahfouz won the Nobel Prize in literature.

port (PORT)—a harbor or place where boats and ships can dock or anchor safely

prime minister (PRIME MIN-uh-stur)—the person in charge of the cabinet in Egypt

republic (ri-PUHB-lik)—a government headed by a president with officials elected by the people

revolution (rev-uh-LOO-shun)—an uprising by the people of a country that attempts to change its system of government

Internet Sites

FactHound offers a safe, fun way to find Internet sites related to this book. All of the sites on FactHound have been researched by our staff.

Here's how:
1. Visit *www.facthound.com*
2. Type in this special code **0736826882** for age-appropriate sites. Or enter a search word related to this book for a more general search.
3. Click on the **Fetch It** button.

FactHound will fetch the best sites for you!

Read More

Gray, Shirley W. *Egypt.* First Reports. Minneapolis: Compass Point Books, 2002.

Park, Ted. *Taking Your Camera to Egypt.* Austin, Texas: Steadwell Books, 2000.

Zuehlke, Jeffrey. *Egypt in Pictures.* Visual Geography Series. Minneapolis: Lerner, 2003.

Index